Organic Evolution

ORGANIC EVOLUTION

REINVENT AND REJUVENATE EMPLOYEE RESOURCES GROUPS AND OTHER DIVERSITY AND INCLUSION STRATEGIES THROUGH CERTIFICATIONS

Nyah Lynn Edwards

© 2015 Nyah Lynn Edwards
All rights reserved.

ISBN-13: 9780692595510
ISBN-10: 0692595511

Preface

I truly believe in the human spirit coming together and collectively making a change for the betterment of society. I believe that all people should be afforded the opportunity to secure employment and be able to contribute to the best of their abilities. At a very young age I became hugely aware that not everyone is given that opportunity or treated in the same respectful manner.

In the year 1968 Reverend Dr. Martin Luther King Jr., went to Memphis, Tennessee to help sanitation workers receive equity in pay and treatment; two barriers that impede full inclusion still today. Many people forget or were not aware that Dr. King died engaging in attempts to move American workplaces from an awareness of diversity to practicing full workplace inclusion. While he was a pioneer in diversity and inclusion, those two deeply connected words are rarely uttered next to his name. I was all of 13 years old and American workplaces piqued my interest as a new frontier for me.

Fast-forward to 1999, at that time I was employed with Illinois Power and tasked with leading our diversity and Equal Employment Opportunity (EEO) initiatives. Illinois Power, or IP as it was known back then was the second largest gas, electric and nuclear company in the state of Illinois at that time. It was a challenging and invigorating time in my career. The utility industry by and large was a "good old-boys" club but it was changing, diversifying due in part to public outcry for deregulation.

However, in many ways the utility industry as a whole remained draconian, for instance, in how quickly it evolved in recognizing inclusion of all people as an asset. Though many of the barriers of inclusion were coming down, we were able to put together a "Champions of Diversity Program" (as many organizations did and still do) in addition to developing and implementing Employee Resource Groups throughout several regions. Ultimately the company started Illinova University, an internal school led by Dr. Phil Carey a gregarious intellect, thought-leader and collaborator. With his newly created strategy, all company training and education would be designed and presented in-house. Carey was quite interested in working with Diversity and Inclusion and I was elated. He understood and was willing to take the necessary steps to keep our human capital in the forefront of performance and valuing all people. Together, in collaboration with our direct reports we would construct training for all people processes. Wow! I was ready. Alas, it was not to be.

Illinova University lifespan was short lived in part because of reorganization and others felt our thinking was "out there." I felt limited as many of the forward thinking leaders who coached, mentored and developed me "the good, good old boys", took early retirement. I elected to stretch myself instead of fitting within the limiting box I was now being tasked with. I had a need to diversify my knowledge and skillset if I were to follow in the footsteps of those who thought outside of the box of bridging people, processes and opportunities. I left my company, a difficult decision because in many ways this was family, and struck out on my own to put my formal education into practical application.

In 2003 I found myself subcontracting with Ford Motor Company on their initial companywide diversity training. I had the privilege to work with Dr. Chris J. Metzler, a brilliant legal mind and thought leader and also other professionals. It was during this time that discussions first surfaced to present the course to a university for certification. We were all so excited about the possibilities. Metzler worked diligently though unfortunately the idea fell through. The seed remained planted in my organizational mindset and grew exponentially.

My dear colleague and friend Mark Bombaci and I rejoined forces in 2013 and 2014 to develop a Diversity Certification Training that he would present for George Washington University his alma mater. Mark and I had worked together at Ford Motor Company, becoming close friends and colleagues when we completed the contract after many of the consultants fled when the company we were contracting with went bankrupt, leaving most of us unpaid. I searched through my old notepapers on my thoughts about creating internal certification processes for diversity and inclusion and other management and leadership practices and started revamping my ideas and key concepts.

In 2015, I implemented a test pilot through an organization to implement a small portion of the certification concept. A well-known company and client, who will remain confidential, approached me about working with them on putting together a Champions of Inclusion Program. I introduced my concept of a certification process for each employee resources group stressing its global applicability. Initially the director was not overly joyed about the concept. After speaking with others she came back elated and said, "My Champions of Inclusion Program will be a certification program." I was given the go ahead to integrate the Champions of Inclusion Program into my concept of a certification process. The certification program has been well received by the organization, and is viewed as a competitive advantage and I predict that it will become a "Best Practice," not for the sake of best practices but because it is what current organizational needs demand.

Within these pages you will find that this book is about concepts, theories and practical applications. I draw upon some of the great minds of organizational theories and concepts including the works of Abraham Maslow, Frederick Winslow Taylor, Marilyn Loden and Judy B. Rosener and Peter F. Drucker and others to illustrate past, present and future connections to organizational culture and the people working within the system.

Certifications are not new but you already know that though. The application that I conceived and offer to you uses an old concept in a new way. Why I believe that this process will be accepted today compared to yesterdays gone by are simple, timing and a mind shift. In the past, most could not conceive of online universities, the mere thought was rejected out of hand. Yet today online higher learning from reputable universities is a reality. In that vein, this book is a conceptually new "Best Practices" born out of the organic evolution of Employee Resource Groups and overall Employee Development training.

Be Inspired and Inspiring!
Nyah

Acknowledgements

I owe a debt of gratitude to a great deal of individuals who with their support, kindness and encouragement has propelled me throughout the years. There is no way possible to list each and every one. I do want you to know that I am very appreciative of any and all things that you have said and done to assist me in my endeavors. I would like to acknowledge a few individuals in particular.

Mark Bombaci and Judy Jourdain Earl are always open to hearing my organizational theories, concepts and people strategies. Mark and Judy will ask the same question fifty ways and in doing so forces one to think about ideas full circle. Mark will write and rewrite – wordsmith you to death, but I am exhausted and exhilarated by the finished product. Judy is a talker and she will talk you up, over and around a thought and when she finishes the thought has truly become a masterpiece. I am much appreciative to count both Mark and Judy as friends and collaborators.

I work with several American organizations and I have met quite a number of standup and standout people in each of them. Without exception, I would like to acknowledge Sodexo USA Office of Diversity Leadership for allowing me to consult and train within their organization for over ten years now. Our partnership has allowed me to observe their Employee Resource Groups (ERG) interactions, develop key trainings for their ERG Signature Programs, and other companywide initiatives including the Spirit of Inclusion and much more. In particular special thank you to Phillip Edge, Jodi Davidson, Denise Ammaccapane and former Sodexo employees Kim Weaver, Cecy Kuruvilla, Betsy Silva Hernandez and Dr. Bryan Gingrich who were courageous and instrumental in challenging the organization to become more inclusive.

Table of Contents

Historical Journey 1

    Organizational Theories and Historical Context 3

    Abraham Maslow Hierarchy 6

The People Factor 13

    Emergent Workforce – They're Here... 15

Current ERG Structures and Focus 19

    Current Employee Resources Groups Structure and Focus 21

    SWOT Analysis 25

    Separate Equal and Flawed? 26

A Shift in Focus 35

    Rethinking and Advancing Inclusion and Diversity Training 37

The Business Case for Certifications · 41

        Benefits · 43

Certification Processes · 45

        Certification Credentialing Concepts · · · · · · · · · · · · · · · · 47

Low Hanging Fruit · 67

        Value-Added Actions · 69

Epilogue · 75

About the Author · 77

Historical Journey

In this section we look at management and sociologist theorists and their theories and concepts that shaped our past and future.

Organizational Theories and Historical Context

Diversity and Inclusion (D&I) Training and Employee Resources Groups (ERGs) are a natural outgrowth of workplace systems that seek peak performance from their human capital in a highly competitive market. Many foundational, historical concepts are clearly evident in current Diversity & Inclusion (D&I)[1] strategies, management and leadership concepts and organizational design. Many of these strategies materialized from their predecessors. Here are but a few examples of how and why organizations evolved to where we are currently.

Frederick Winslow Taylor (1856 – 1915) came into prominence during the industrialization age. Taylor is regarded as the father of modern management. In addition to being a mechanical engineer he also become one of the first management consultants to organizations.

Taylor organically applied his skills in engineering to his philosophies of the workplace. Taylorism, as it is called include "analysis; synthesis; logic, rationality, empiricism; work ethic; efficiency and elimination of waste; and standardization of best practices."[2]

Though many still follow Taylor's scientific method today, during his day a great number of his peers opposed his concepts as they lacked consideration for the human factor. Scientific management peaked in the 1910s and faded a decade later in the 1920s due to competing theories.

---
1 Diversity will proceed the word inclusion when the emphasis is placed on differences as opposed to inclusion
2 en.wikipedia.org/wiki/scientific-management#Taylor27s-view-of-workers

3

When Taylor developed his concepts he was working within an industrialization landscape and the main focus was machinery. However, we are no longer operating within this environment. In comparison to Taylor's days to our current work environment the human factor is the *IT* factor. When we look at the scientific method through diversity and inclusion lens, what remains useful and productive from Taylorism, is the standardization of best practices, analysis and synthesizes of people practices (not just merely the workplace). As the adage goes, "we should not throw away the baby with the bath water." Thus, it is the synthesis of people practices where ERG certifications will shine brightly and usher continuous change.

Quality Circles, first introduced in the 1960s became prominent in the 1980s. In a nutshell, Quality Circles are a group of employee formed teams who meet during predetermined company times, who do the same or similar type work to identify and analyze work issues and offer solutions. Quality Circles members were usually prohibited from speaking on company issues such as terms of condition of employment. Many people erroneously contributed the Quality Circles movement to Dr. W. Edwards Deming (more background on Deming provided within the next few pages). However, Professor Kaoru Ishikawa introduced and coined its conception in his 1988 handbook, "What is Total Quality Control?" Nippon Wireless and Telegraph Company (Japanese Company) were the first to introduce the concept into industry in 1962.

In a real sense Employee Resources Groups are an outgrowth of Quality Circles. ERG members gather to discuss issues pertaining to specific characteristics i.e., sexual orientation, religion and so forth. Where ERGs differ from Quality Circles, the real distinction, is that ERGs do discuss terms and conditions of employment with the exception of labor concerns. Employees may nonetheless discuss policies that are deemed "Best Practices" for other companies and discuss its merits both pros and cons. The goal of ERGs is to aid in the creation of an inclusive culture whereas people can bring their best to the organization to enhance the performance of the organization and the individual. Hence, organizations evolved to gaining a better understanding of the human factor and how conditions impact people. There is no better explanation of this phenomenon than the one brought forth in the "hierarchy of needs."

Abraham Maslow (1908 – 1970), an American psychologist and creator of his iconic hierarchy of needs. Many believe that Maslow most likely drew upon his own life experiences (socialization) of being the "other," as he was the only Jewish boy in his childhood neighborhood. As the saying goes, "necessity is the mother of invention" and one can feel real experience, understanding and wisdom within each level of his hierarchy of needs. This concept is about humanity plain and simple. Regardless of our diversity each and every one of us falls within each level of Maslow's concept. That is why his concept is just as relevant today as it was when Maslow first introduced this concept. Hierarchy of needs encompasses individual, group, and organizational levels and it can be viewed as a pantheon for ERGs.

Abraham Maslow Hierarchy

Maslow Hierarchy	Organizational Applications
Physiological Needs Food, water, warmth, rest	Employable and gainfully employed; breaks both mental and physical
Safety Needs Security and Safety	Policies against workplace violence and harassment and Safety Policies
Belonging Needs Relationships, friends, peers and cohorts	Employee Resource Groups, Teams and Teamwork etc.,
Esteem Needs Prestige and feelings of accomplishments	Certifications, Employee of the Month, Best Company to Work For, Best in Class etc.,
Self-Actualization Needs Achieving one's full potential	Living | Working in Purpose

Equally as important, if you overlay the goals, objectives and mission of most employee resources group you will find that each level of Maslow's needs is embedded within ERGs initiatives. Some might argue that the physiological needs are not included, I would counter, and it depends on how you look at it. I believe that there is a direct relationship between employment, food, and water, wouldn't you agree?

Self-Actualization continues to be on the forefront of most people today. In fact, when you hear diversity and inclusion professionals, life coaches, motivational speakers, and spiritual and religious leaders speak on finding one's purpose they are directly speaking about finding and being all that you were meant to be or in other words: self-actualization. Is it possible to reach the pinnacle of your being within the workforce? Dr. Edward R. Demining thinks so.

Dr. Edward R. Deming (1900 – 1993) offered great insights into gaining access into the collective knowledge of the organization's members. In his critically acclaimed book, *Out of the Crisis*, he outlined 14 management points aimed at creating an efficient workplace, glean higher profits and increase productivity.

Deming's 14 Points
1. Create and communicate to all employees a statement of the aims and purposes of the company.
2. Adapt to the new philosophy of the day; industries and economics are always changing.
3. Build quality into a product throughout production.
4. End the practice of awarding business on the basis of price tag alone; instead, try a long-term relationship based on established loyalty and trust.
5. Work to constantly improve quality and productivity.
6. Institute on-the-job training.
7. Teach and institute leadership to improve all job functions.
8. Drive out fear; create trust
9. Strive to reduce intradepartmental conflicts.
10. Eliminate exhortations for the work force; instead, focus on the system and morale.

11. (a) Eliminate work standard quotas for production. Substitute leadership methods for improvement.
    (b) Eliminate Managing By Objectives (MBO). Avoid numerical goals. Alternatively, learn the capabilities of processes, and how to improve them.
12. Remove barriers that rob people of pride of workmanship.
13. Educate with self-improvement programs.
14. Include everyone in the company to accomplish the transformation.

As you read through the points you can see how they reflect many employee resources groups as well as most companies' strategic initiatives for inclusion. Several of Deming's 14 points will be highlighted in future chapters. I would be remiss if I did not draw your attention to point ten. In current workplace environments, it behooves us to exhort the workforce, focus on the system and morale. People want us to appeal to their needs as much as the needs of the company. Both can coexist. Think back to Abraham Maslow's hierarchy of needs you can see that as much and as often change occurs some things remain the same. The overlap of theories is evident. There is always an overlap or a new starting point for a concept or philosophical thinker. One of the greatest philosophical thinkers for management and leadership to date was Peter F. Drucker.

Drucker's (1909 – 2005) writings and teachings were greatly influenced by Frederick Winslow Taylor and others. Drucker considered "the founder of modern management" explored management as an author and renowned consultant. His writings and concepts are as influential today as they were when he wrote them. "Management is doing things right; leadership is doing the right things," he often quipped and others continue to quote him today.

If you have read any (or all) of Drucker's books and juxtapose them against the time period that he wrote them you might wonder, like others, where he hid his tarot cards or crystal ball. Many of his predictions, though not all, came to fruition, as examples "privatization, and decentralization, the rise of Japan to economic world power, the end of the blue-collar worker, and the emergence of the information society all came to fruition. Of course we know that he didn't have a crystal ball or tarot cards. What he had was a laser focused brain and capitalized his thoughts on people, on relationships, on a need for community (overlapping Abraham Maslow) and the ever-evolving society. As I stated earlier, Drucker was not always correct in his predictions, he was said to be loose with facts at times. In my humble opinion, we should not look for perfection but for humanists, those who put people over things including title. For true humanists realize that valuing people will bring you the very things that the company desires, outstanding performance and success.

And ultimately that is what the concepts here embody dealing with where we are as a people, where we are going, and what processes and intellect will propel us, and how we garner the people factor to move us closer to a more inclusive workplace. Facing our organizations with a mindset of meeting today's needs and expectations is crucial to survival. Organizations' and its stakeholders must walk in integrity, grace and courage and shift when needed.

What is truly admirable about Drucker, for my part, is his courage to speak and stand in truths the way he saw it. He drew fire from one of the largest most influential companies at the time GM, when he gave feedback about the organization's management style. It will take courage for every member in the organization to stand in their truth and give voice when processes, leadership and a culture is not working, especially when a great deal of resources, time, money and people have been poured into an initiative that really need serious tweaking. We must get it right.

Former president George W. Bush certainly got it right on July 9, 2002 when he awarded Drucker the Presidential Medal of Freedom. Freedom to contribute to an organization (overlapping Dr. MLK Jr. and the sanitation workers actions) is one of the most important freedoms for mankind (Maslow's self-actualization). People and systems are ever evolving. We can easily see visual changes including technological and demographical variations. Yet, are we changing at the pace that is required to be operationally sound in today's global atmosphere?

In 1991 Marilyn Loden and Judy B. Rosener wrote a game-changing book, "Workforce America!" In this book they talked about the impact of history on American organizations and the shifting demographics of future America (of course these shifts are occurring around the world).

One of the most philosophical concepts that Loden and Rosener brought to life is the model explaining the dimensions of diversity. Some practitioners refer to the model as the "Diversity Wheel." Many companies use some iteration of this model to discuss the multilayer dimensions of people diversity. Hence, I will not provide an illustration within these pages. What I will point out is that this book is continues to be very valid. It is a book that I suggest leaders and members should read and reread and apply it to the current landscape that we face.

Namely, the authors candidly discuss demographics and the implications of shifting demographics, culture clashes, and assimilation and a myriad of barriers that people who are "other" face, and continue to face I might add. They also speak on leveraging differences, seeing differences as assets rather than problems. They speak on topics that are not going away, many people items that we are confronted with may morph and emerge a little differently, because people dynamics shift and many ways they stay the same. What remains the same is that people want to be respected, valued and provided opportunities to share their gifts and talents. The latter, respect, value and opportunity, will always remain as the brass ring (though there will be nuances) because our needs is about the human factor.

Most organizations and its members will attest that it is not enough just to have diversity representation in the organization. Most members, if not most leaders, will attest that it is not enough to follow *Best Practices* as part of a condition of being rote. *Best Practices* is not just about information. It is not merely about classroom exercises. Rather *Best Practices* is a broad concept and must be based on sound doctrine. We must consistently seek to move our people processes forward. I suggest that internal certifications are the latest-game changers to respond to our changing landscape within all organizations.

The People Factor

In this section we review shifting demographics, employees' needs and the abilities of organizations to continuously shift to meet these needs.

Emergent Workforce – They're Here...

Looking back, Y2k predictions were scary! The scariest, by far, that computer networks would crash creating mass destruction as we were connected worldwide. In reality there were a few scatter computer glitches in Y2k but dire predictions did not materialize. What did materialize and went mostly unnoticed from the masses ushered in a new order so to speak in the U.S.

In the year 2000 the U.S. Census Bureau allowed people to choose more than one category to describe who they are. It caused some debate, particularly within the black community fears that this was a tool to once again marginalize a people who experienced multitudes of exclusion. Nonetheless, whether you agree or disagree the change in census identification withstood the controversy. This change to the U.S. census reflected changing sentiments, philosophies about race in America.

From the inception of the change to the census data category to 2010, people who identified themselves as multiracial grew substantially. Couple this with the fact that there is an increase in multiracial births creates one of the largest and newest landscape changes to the marketplace. In 1970 multiracial births represented a mere 1% of all birth, in 2013 that percentage increased to 10%. The multiracial experience in and of itself may differ from either experience of one subset racial group of a multiracial individual. Meaning, being multiracial – though people may associate you based on how you look, may not necessarily bring about the same experiences of those of one race of an individual's lineage. This is not the only major shift.

One of the greatest shifts in demographics is in the category of age occurring worldwide. Traditionalists, those born before 1946[3] are scarcely in the workforce or in society. Sadly, we are losing this generation rapidly. The baby boomers (boomers), those born between the years of 1946 - 1964 have now moved into the elder ranks. As you may have heard, as of 2010 each day 10,000 boomers will turn the age of sixty-five. It is now 2015 and we are edging towards 2016. That impact is evident as millennials, those born between the years of 1981- 2000, as of 2015, now outnumber boomers as the largest living age group in the United States. Boomers also want to feel valued and not seen as waiting for their time to lapse. And due, in no small part, to the economy many are reinventing themselves to meet today's employment challenges and opportunities. As boomers begin to consider retirement or have retired, as they consider their latter stages in life they want to remain active and current. Whether boomers work beyond what has been viewed as the norm for retirement age or not, it will be beneficial for boomers to grow in human relations skills needed for the current environment. Certifications can meet boomers needs.

Generation X, those born between the years of 1965-1980 are approximately 25 million fewer than baby boomers. Gen Xers, as they are often called, are expected to do more with less – primarily less resources in the organization. Gen Xers could be called the sandwich generation, a moniker often given to the boomers for being sandwiched between taking care of their kids (or grandkids) and their parents. Yet, in a real sense Gen Xers are sandwiched in between two large groups boomers and millennials two groups who have garnered much more attention. How can organizations create a greater buy-in from Xers when opportunities for promotion may not be as readily available as years past? What used to be touted, as future predictions are today's realities! Lateral moves within organizations are a reality for Xers and thus certifications will meet Xers needs as well.

Millennials, they've arrived and they are quite anxious to conquer the world. They have expectations, desires and realities that have been shaped by previous generations, Xers and Boomers. Millennials are

---

[3] Generation birth date spans may change depending on the expert

confident, assertive and if you happen to work with a millennial, most likely you do, you know that most will make their needs known. Some of those needs are to spend more time with family and friends, work to live. Some people call them "Generation Me," indicating negativity rather than "Generation Me," taking stock of my whole self, all of my needs including my purpose and my drive. Like it or not, unlike boomers, whom self-focus was a new concept, it is not a new concept for millennials nor will it be for future generations. Self-focus and balance will continue to show up in humanity in various ways including work-life balance and workforce health programs. Millennials and Xers are now more than ever in the driver seat and driving further, rapidly into the future. Organizations must meet the needs of its newest workforce culture. Certifications will boost learning for millennials while lessening time away from social and home life, providing what they expect, work/life balance.

You've hired the best and brightest Xers and millennials and you've successfully retained boomers. What's next? Experts note that retention will be key for employers as research has shown that the average tenure for millennials is two years. That being said, the worldwide economic landscape may slow this trend down a tad but retention is still key. How will you retain those who are poised to shape this newly created frontier?

We retain our human resources by offering services and products designed to fit current employees' needs and current environmental needs. One offering is to show value to continuous education that will benefit the organization and all future members as well. Certifications then are a current win-win strategy, a best practice, and an organic evolution.

Current ERG Structures and Focus

This section delves into the current landscape, acknowledging what are currently being done well, what can be done better and methods to infuse the two.

Current Employee Resources Groups Structure and Focus

Up to this point I have provided background information as to why and how employee resources groups came into being. Equally as important is how employee resources groups (ERG) are structured and their focus.

Most ERGs continued to be structured as silos[4]. These silos are focused around various dimensions of humanity including but not limited to (listed alphabetically) age, disabilities, gender, generations, race (5 or more racial groups), sexual orientation and veterans. Some organizations are beginning to include faith.

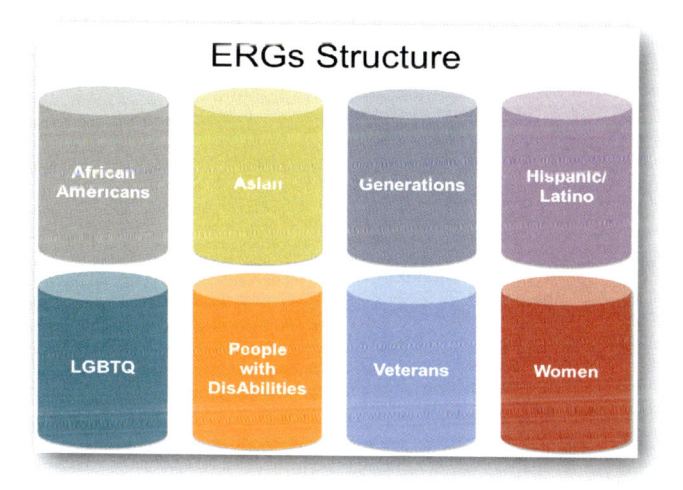

ERGs Structure

- African Americans
- Asian
- Generations
- Hispanic/Latino
- LGBTQ
- People with DisAbilities
- Veterans
- Women

---
4 ERGs are listed alphabetically in the model

ERGs usually have a charter, a mission, and an executive sponsor. They are usually provided a budget, whether it is adequate or not will not be part of the discussions in this book. Indeed, as a reminder, employee resources groups are similar to Quality Circles of the 1980s with a few caveats. ERGs invariably speak on company policies and culture. They bring to the attention of leadership direct and indirect business needs. They offer recommendations to include various policies to attract and retain diverse employees. They, like Quality Circles, refrain from discussing specific personnel issues between management and an individual and avoid interfering with labor/union rights. ERGs are and will continue to be a powerful asset to organizations.

DiversityInc, the premiere organization that analyzes and recognizes the efforts of companies for diversity inclusion released their 2015 listing of the best companies for ERGs[5]. DiversityInc, reports that they compile their listing based on the following criteria:

- "Whether groups have formal charters
- Percentage of employees in at least one group
- Racial/gender breakdown of groups
- Percentage of top executives who are sponsors of groups
- Whether groups are used for recruitment, on-boarding of new employees, talent development, marketing, mentoring and diversity training.
- If groups success is measured through retention, engagement, talent development and other contributions to business (focus groups client interactions, marketing ideas)
- If resource group leaders have national positions in executive diversity councils."

Being recognized as a leader in ERGs is not only an honor and privilege it is representative of the diligence of the collective energies and effort put forth by employees and leaders. The existence of ERGs is vital to bridging relationships and valuing people.

---

[5] www.diversityinc.com/top-10-company-employee-resource-groups/

I am reminded of traveling with my son in the car, driving from Champaign, IL to Tiptonville, TN, and he would say, "Mom, are we there yet?" I would reply, "no, not yet!"

The same can be said with organizational goals seeking to become fully inclusive, we're not there yet. In fact, we will never *fully* know all that we need to know because humans adapt and evolve organically. In short, we'll never totally be there. Humans are kinetic. That's the beauty of being human we always have the ability within our reach to shift and change. The best employee resources groups do are to bring us closer to the realization of being vitally inclusive doing the best with what we know now. Employee resources groups serve that purpose. Recognizing the accomplishments of all employee resources groups is paramount to galvanizing a collective mindset of inclusion.

DiversityInc Top 10 Companies for Employee Resource Groups for 2015 are:

1. Merck & Co
2. EY
3. PricewaterhouseCoopers
4. Dell
5. KPMG
6. AT&T
7. Novartis Pharmaceuticals Corporation
8. Kellogg Company
9. MasterCard
10. Caterpillar

This is certainly an impressive listing. I am sure the listing of those companies who did not make the top ten listing is equally as impressive.

When we truly care about inclusion we not only recognize milestones but we must become hyper vigilant in noticing flaws in our processes and practices. When we can do this with a mindset and heart of improvement we can continue onward towards individual, group and organizational rewards of inclusion and value. One of the best tools to assist in this discovery is the SWOT Analysis – Strengths, Weaknesses, Opportunities and Threats will provide insights into all processes and practices of ERGS and at a minimum reveal missed opportunities. Though this tool is not new, it may quite possible be one of the most underutilized, straightforward, and cost-efficient resource available.

SWOT Analysis

Strengths, Weaknesses, Opportunities and Threats

Annually, each ERG should perform an analysis on their membership development and companywide outreach development and discuss. This is a very crucial step in a process as top issues for social groups (diversity characteristics) may change and thus focuses are consistently shifting. This will be discussed in greater detail in the training section.[6]

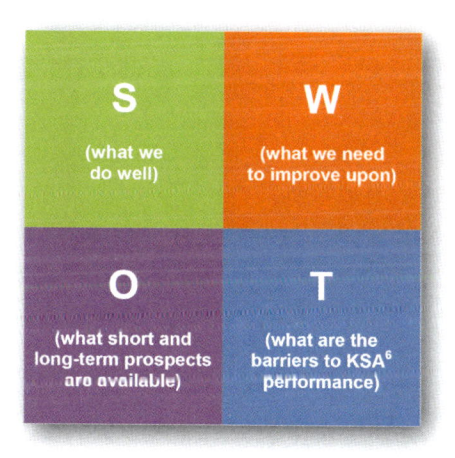

S (what we do well)	W (what we need to improve upon)
O (what short and long-term prospects are available)	T (what are the barriers to KSA[6] performance)

Using this model there is are key humanity areas that most organizational areas focus on exceptionally well and there are some key areas where there is a shortfall.

---
6 KSA=Knowledge, Skills and Abilities

Separate Equal and Flawed?

The landmark United States Supreme 1964 case Brown v. the Board of Education in Topeka, Kansas demonstrated that separate but equal really had major flaws. The Supreme Court ruled that de jure racial discrimination was a violation of the fourteenth amendment. This ruling spurred integration, assimilation and anticipation. What does separate but equal have to do with ERGs? There is parallel between the two.

In reality ERGs have a valid necessity to have groupings focused on certain dimensions of humanity. Having ERGs grouped around these characteristics benefits the organization and its members and members at large. Working in dedicated groups focused on specific concerns and opportunities creates an atmosphere of comfort, of safety for full disclosure, of belonging, of understanding and clarity (Maslow's Hierarchy). It also ensures valid issues do not fall through the cracks. I am very supportive of ERGs. It is my desire to see them evolve and keep pace with the needs of the people they serve. In order to fully do that we must be willing to capitalize on what we do well and become more willing and able to expose flaws.

Where ERGs lack is the confluence between the dimensions that represent the whole person. In other words, there is a huge flaw operationally in the design (slightly) and the implementation (to a larger degree) of ERGs. This flaw creates stagnation and is limiting. Much like separate and unequal precepts and integration here in the United States.

Humans are not solely one thing or another. We have more than one characteristic operating *simultaneously* and each of our characteristics is important to us. Each ERGs primarily focus on one dimension of diversity. Improvements for ERGs must be made in addressing two concepts in particular, simultaneity and intersectionality.

Simultaneity

As mentioned earlier, humans are not one thing or another; we have a great many characteristics that are happening at the same time. I will use myself to illustrate this point. I am a woman plus a mother plus a professional plus a dog owner plus a Christian plus...a great many things. It goes on and on like this for each one of us.

Evangelina Holvino, a senior research faculty at Simmons Graduate School of Management defines simultaneity as "Identities and differences are contextual and depending on the situation some dimensions of one's identity come to be figural and others become background."

> *When I'm at work, my professional dimension and characteristics take center stage and my being a mother moves to the background. It doesn't mean that being a mother is less important or not important at all. In fact, if a certain type of telephone call were received involving my son, I would shift my mom dimension to the foreground and move my professional self to the background.*

This example illustrated how simultaneity exists; most of us have an understanding of this concept. What can happen is as we deal with others we can forget that people are made up of a lot of important factors that may be coming into play whether we are attuned to them or not. Within this example I also edged us closer to another concept. When two or more characteristics intersect, as is said, shift happens.

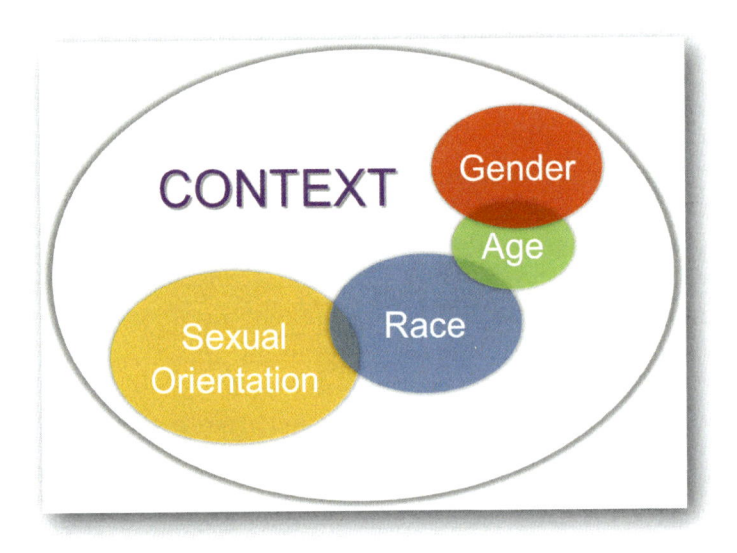

Intersectionality

We all belong to various social groups. Some of us belong to the women group, and others belong to the men group. Some of us belong to the millennial group and other belongs to the GenX group. Some belong to the Caucasian group and others belong to other racial groups and so forth. As simultaneity clearly demonstrates, different social group identities that we belong to are not mutually exclusive. And we must not view humans as such. It is worthwhile for organizations to understand how our various characteristics may intersect with one another particularly in the workplace.

Universities, and other higher education institutions understand and readily discuss intersectionality. In comparison, the concept of intersectionality is where most companies fall short. Most ERGs and companies have not woven intersectionality into their strategies or tactical initiatives.

Before I discuss this in more detail I want to first provide an example as an invaluable teachable moment. This is an actual example of course no names will be used. This is a learning tool, not a punishing stick or for us to point fingers.

> *A consultant had been hired by a firm to develop a D&I training on women in the workplace. The very robust training was developed and test piloted. The pilot was well received by the director and a team of other stakeholders from across the company. This training had a historical component to illustrate how the U.S. gender employment evolved to where it is today. The consultant trained a small cadre of external professional facilitators, who each had a minimum of 15 years of experience, on how to facilitate the curriculum and engage internal employees in a Train-the-Trainer session. The external team was then slated to train approximately 30 plus internal facilitators (beginner facilitators for D&I) on how to deliver the course. The internal facilitators are good people, who were committed to driving diversity deeper into the organization. What could go wrong, right? Within five minutes of presenting the Gender Timeline, there was a major disruption in the room. The internal facilitators[7] were aghast that race was included in the timeline. There were only two examples of when race and gender intersected, pay and promotions. Over and over again the internal facilitators lamented, "This has nothing to do with race, this is supposed to be about gender." Ultimately, the internal facilitators refused to facilitate the course, becoming disruptive and argumentative.*

---

7 A few of the minority facilitators of color became visibly uncomfortable and literally tried to become invisible in the room.

What happened, what caused the uproar? There was a collective mindset in the room that all women issues were the same for all women and all men issues were the same for all men. There was an outright rejection of the concept intersectionality. You see the organization had not fully engaged or prepared their internal diversity facilitators beyond awareness, beyond a silo experience and thus these facilitators, who lacked experience of intersectionality, responded accordingly. The aforementioned company focused more on diversity rather than inclusion and thus this contributed to the disconnect. The actions of the internal facilitators can also be attributed to the glib statement being touted in many organizations, "diversity is more than race and gender." Anxious to move past, we may be leaving bodies in the quake.

Actress Patricia Arquette courageously confronted intersectionality when she accepted her 2015 Academy Award for Best Supporting Actress. During her accepting speech she noted the pay differences among women of color and white women in comparison to for every dollar a man makes (it should be white man makes as the average is based on white males) a woman (depending on race) make... The Gender Timeline breaking down pay based on race and gender, promotion based on race and gender, intersectionality, the exact same information Arquette provided was overload for the internal facilitators.

Here is a major flaw. The company in the aforementioned example has had a formal D&I strategy, as many large companies have, for more than ten years. They are very adept at providing silo training, as most companies are, and they fail to move beyond basic inclusion needs. When we ignore intersectionality and simultaneity we are missing a huge mark for ERGs.

It should be noted that some of the employees of color later made comments about the company not really wanting to deal with real or certain issues. When companies work diligently to improve employee relations, and acknowledge diversity and garner inclusion, comments like these are a major blow. This is a crack in the performance for inclusion. This is one of the reasons it is so important for the organization to address intersectionality. Another valid reason is to gauge the nuances within groups to understand communities and market share. This information will assist the organization's brand internally and externally.

Understanding intersectionality beyond an Affirmative Action Plan (AAP), a management tool designed to look at underutilization is a must. AAPs are a good tool but it does not look at the entire scale and scope of how an individual may be impacted on a human level beyond a legal one.

Yet, there are some companies who are courageously delving into intersectionality and are making great strides and positive impacts. Here is a notable mention:

> *Jasmyne McDonald, a Human Resources Project Specialist for Cigna wrote a superlative article for Diversity Best Practices titled, "Millennial Mondays' – How Cigna Leveraged Gen Y to Create a Platform for Inter-Generational Conversations." In this August 25, 2014 article McDonald described the benefits of having intersect identities conversations. The company started an internal blog (Millennial Mondays) that increased enterprise-wide participation. Cigna was able to reach employees who in the past remained silent. After the blog, many of the silent gave power to their voice and engaged in conversations. Cigna tapped into several needs and opportunities. This blog engaged more of the whole person rather than looking at them through the lens of a single dimension of diversity.*

Cigna has nine employee resource groups – unlimited possibilities to delve into intersect conversations and bringing more employees into the game of leveraging company goals and opportunities. Moreover, employees were able to share innovative ideas, network and engage with entry level and mid-level employees, improve communication skills including writing styles and provide insights in the retention of millennials.

Clearly Cigna has taken a closer look at the benefits of meeting the current needs of the organization. They partner technology; interest, motivation and the people factor in a positive amalgamation producing a win-win strategy. Including trainings with intersectionality in mindset will catapult their growth in many ways too.

In later chapters we will highlight in more details how ERGs can breathe life into bringing an understanding of intersectionality to their organizations while elevating thinking and alleviating some valid concerns of stakeholders and producing positive outcomes.

A short list of other intersectionality examples may include age and disabilities; gender and sexual orientation, LGBT equality across race, LGBT equality across generations, generations and work/life balance, race and gender, race and language, sexual orientation and religion and so much more.

ORGANIC EVOLUTION

For now, here is an illustration of intersectionality in the human experience that may show up in the workplace in on-boarding, wages, position, promotion, credibility, respect or lack thereof, productivity and commitment:

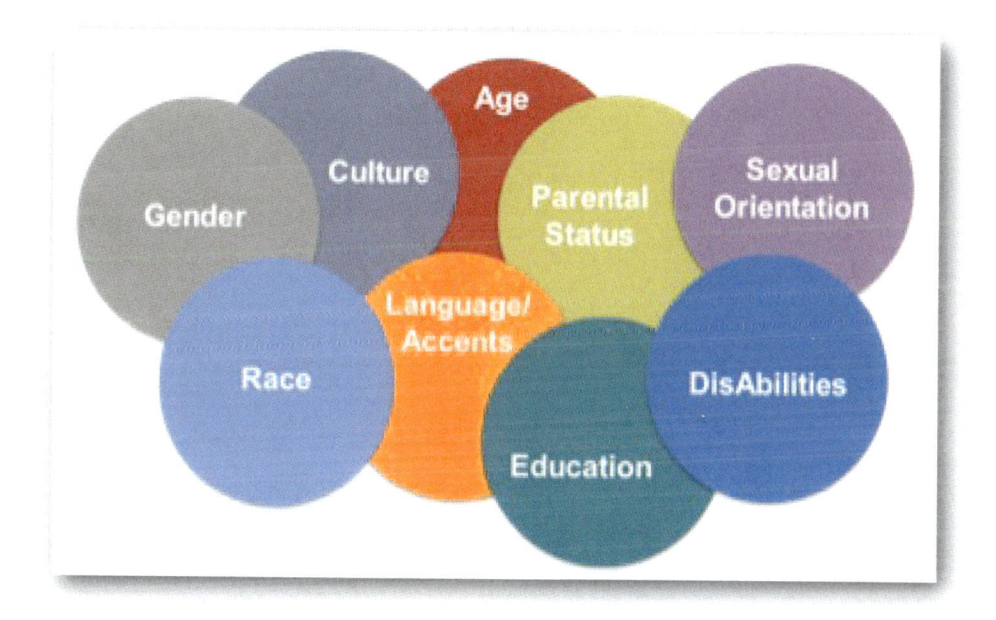

33

A Shift in Focus

In this section we examine efforts and rethink current emphasis and evolve from awareness of diversity to immersion of inclusion of diversity.

Rethinking and Advancing Inclusion and Diversity Training

Leading, managing, counseling, coaching and inclusion are all important elements to the success of the organization. Quite frankly, if your role is far enough away from the top tier and closer to entry level, employees may not be aware of how they play into the success of an fully integrated (all facets), inclusive organization. Although...a number of entry-level employees believe they are faced with diversity more so than mid-to upper levels. That may be the case for race and gender diversity, statistical data bears that out, but it is not necessarily the case for many other characteristics of diversity.

No matter what level people may find themselves in the organization, most people want to be successful. Most people want to contribute fully and most times above and beyond their roles, closer to whom they are rather than whom their title tethers them to be. Some people will take roles just to get in the door as they scout out the positions that they truly want. It behooves organizations to have a clear-cut path to educating and training employees on inclusion at all levels. If we are training them anyway, why not certify their learning?

All employees are expected to stay up-to-date on safety rules and regulations. To ensure a safety culture, employees are trained and in some instances certified (CPR) to affirm proficiency. Apprentices are required to have a strategy to execute and verify their learning and guidelines on how to remain up-to-date on requisite skills, and they should. Yet supervisors, managers and executives are expected to manage diverse relationships, an essential function for each of these roles, and yet many organizations do not have in place a strategy plan to ensure that D&I *learning* is taking place. Sure, they are able to quantify who attended what workshop and who has not attended (check the box mindset). Organizations usually provide evaluation forms of what attendees liked and did not like – what worked and what did not work from an audience member's perspective. Overall, there is lack when it comes to providing assessments to ensure *learning* has taken place. If organizational mindsets have not evolved in ensuring learning they ultimately fall short in showing connectivity for deeper continuous learning and understanding.

It is from this point that I will shift and use the terms I&D (including differences, emphasis on inclusion) from D&I (differences and inclusion) as the latter places the emphasis more so on differences). Moreover, though I do not delve deeper into this thought within this book, inclusion training must eventually be connected to job descriptions and promotional advancement at a deeper level. The best way to do this is through internal certifications. The attainment of certifications offer continued, intellectual, professional and personal growth.

Might I suggest that all inclusion and diversity training (learning) should be designed and implemented with an inclusion certification process mindset? Key concepts and other prerequisites to enhance organizational performance and employee needs should be highly regarded and incentivized. Training employees is a form of incentives. Here is what I mean.

According to Wikipedia, McDonald's Center of Excellence was founded in 1961. McDonald's Center of Excellence has trained and graduated in excess of 80,000 restaurant managers and owner/operators from Hamburger University. McDonald's has a lot of firsts including being the first restaurant company to develop a global training center. In addition, they have also received college credit recommendations from American Council on Education (ACE) United States oldest and regarded as the most influential higher education association. That is outstanding. All organizations must begin to focus their efforts on being a knowledge, performance culture more so than ever (global competition). To do this, every company does not need to establish a university to invest into their talent.

"If we are going to go anywhere, we're got to have talent, and; I'm going to put my money in talent."

—Ray Kroc, McDonald's Founder

Here is a radical idea for thought-leaders. Where possible for D&I training designed specifically for leaders, partner with external continuous education programs or professional education institutions. Engage the institution in a conversation to certify internally designed training curriculum under the external certification organization's umbrella.

This way, your organization minimizes costs by not tying monetary investments to brick and mortar for a corporate university. Instead your organization can partner, rebuild, or rewrite your relationships with standalone university programs and continuing education entities already in existence while providing cogent, doable skills to enhance performance of leaders that are nationally and globally recognized.

The cost of most external certification processes ranges anywhere from $2,000 per person to $14,000. For this reason most organizations may find it to be cost prohibitive to enroll each and every member or all leaders within the organization. Moreover, most of the aforementioned programs are usually designed for individuals who want to lead D&I strategies. Internal certification processes seek to raise the bar in leveraging inclusion and driving a higher learning culture.

The Business Case for Certifications

This section identifies accompanying benefits of a certification process on individual, group and organizational levels.

Benefits

In a real sense the benefits of the business case was covered in the demographic overview. I need not provide you a drawn out business case for ERGs, you have already moved beyond that measure if you have ERGs or any diversity initiatives. Rather, here in this section is a summary overview, additional highlights of the benefits for a certification process and its importance of making any and all efforts meaningful. As you read through, you yourself will readily identify others.

Certifications meet the needs of all employees and thus the organizations. Other benefits of certifications include…

1. Meet Abraham Maslow's hierarchy of needs and embed individuals more firmly in self-actualization;
2. Emphasize several of Deming's key points on a higher level including (a) adapt to the new philosophy of the day [greater emphasis on including others organically] (b) work to constantly improve quality and productivity [quality of life and innovation] (c) institute on-the-job-training [specifically experiential opportunities] (d) remove barriers that rob people of pride of workmanship [fear, (e) educate with self-improvement programs [certifications] and (f) include everyone in the company to accomplish the transformation;
3. Creation of sustainable strategies that meet or support company goals and tactics that are accessible to all employees;

4. Provide additional means to benchmark performance of ERGs and individual contributors while connecting skillsets to job roles;
5. Create experiential learning (self and others) and growth opportunities;
6. Build people skills and qualifications for present and future positions;
7. Meet and exceed organizational strategies and tactical needs;
8. Create a culture of life long learners while increasing employee engagement;
9. Members learn practical skills and knowledge with an emphasis on transference to day-to-day operations and the ability to demonstrate what is learned;
10. Add to the creation of a culture of equity;
11. Affordable;
12. Timely;
13. Promotes work/life balance
14. Global applicability – companies with ERGs and diversity initiatives globally can adapt this process worldwide. Improves global dexterity for the organization as well;
15. Self-pace certifications – Convenient and ensures accountability and responsibility for learning on employee; and
16. Leveraging all systems and ERGs – move beyond silo thinking and behaving.

CERTIFICATION PROCESSES

This section provides models, concepts and practices to embed inclusion further into the organization through credentialing.

Certification Credentialing Concepts

The next several pages represent several models that reflect many of the concepts discussed up to this point and essentially bring the certification credentialing concepts to life. I must restate here that certifications are not a new concept. Rather it is applying previous concepts in a new way to assist with the organic growth of ERGs and ever changing needs that will reinvigorate or spur growth. *Your organization may elect to implement one or all of the concepts.*

In most instances certifications should be engaged on a voluntary basis otherwise the company might experience a great deal of casual contempt. *There are two instances that I highly recommend training to be required one is for those who hold leadership, managers and supervisors roles* (shortly you will be introduced to the other). These individuals are tasked with leading, managing and developing the company culture. By nature they create touch points or flashpoints, they will grow or stifle the culture – this is hugely important. Leaders, managers and supervisors are human (sometimes people forget this), they make similar errors involving humanity yet they will often, or should be, held to a higher standard. Let's set every leader up for success rather than hope for it.

Concept 1 – Companywide D&I Certification Process for Leadership, management and supervisors an internal certification credentialed externally or internally. This certification process is for current or future D&I training for those who hold leadership, management and supervisors roles.

Concept 2 – Employee Resource Groups Certification Process
this concept borrows upon certification processes of The Girls Scouts (remember earning those badges) The Boys Scouts and Toastmasters. Certify concepts, theories, and experiences that each participant gains and demonstrate through transference to the workplace. Certifications could be part of a signature program; a training that distinguishes the mission and goal of each ERG or it could be a standalone certification. If you offer different levels within an ERG you may want to establish prerequisites as well i.e., you must complete level I & II before engaging in level III. Certifications for I&D fulfill the mission of ERGs. It is noteworthy to mention that ERGs certification increases participation levels for every group and across the organizational landscape. Careful consideration must be given to the number and duration of activities each ERG will offer in order to keep the momentum going and minimize the potential of becoming "old hat".

Concept 3 – Internal Facilitators Certification Process this concept provides effective, requisite skills for every internal trainer who will be tasked with facilitating inclusion and diversity. Facilitating humanity issues requires different skills then safety training, management and leadership training and most other type training. People are vulnerable when they open themselves up and thus a facilitator must have the requisite skills and adequate training to engage D&I. Therefore, *a certification process for internal facilitators must be a prerequisite to human diversity facilitation.* The more difficult[8] the subject matter, more training should be required.

Concept 4 – ERGs Intersectionality and Simultaneity Certifications Process in this series ERGs are required to partner to develop and implement a certification process with another ERG. Example pairings could be: Women ERG and African Americans ERG (what it means to be a black woman in the organization or society) or Latino (what it means to

---

[8] Some characteristics of diversity requires a highly, qualified individual. In addition, careful consideration must be given in how and who (internal or external) will facilitate

be a Latina woman in the organization or society) ERG or GLBT (what it means to be gay and a millennial) ERG and so forth. This series creates collaboration, acknowledgement of intersectionality and simultaneity and experiential and other learning. Consider this, when playing any electronic games as you progress to the next level of the course your skill levels must become more proficient in order to reach the next level. This certification is designed in that vein, seeking a deeper level of understanding and then applying the learning to the workplace. Additionally, certification credentialing engages ERGs members on higher levels by connecting intersectionality and simultaneity and stretches growth for lifelong learners.

Concept 5 – Capstones in this series, as with educational institutions, specifically in masters programs, capstones are the culminating study. This is where participants, in this case, participants, demonstrate all that is learned through assessments or some other form of quantifying learning.

Concept 1: Companywide D&I Training Certification Process

This template is for credentialing current or future D&I leadership training. The goal of this type certification credentialing[9] is for the learning certificate to be eligible for continuing education credits, or used in the applications for higher education or towards an accredited degree or can be listed solely as a credentialed certification for the employee's own self-actualization.

---

9 There are accredited universities who accept Life Experiences towards credits. These universities will apply credits gained from work training and rather than take a course the student must pass an assessment. As examples Western Governors University, Liberty University and Strayer University offer credit for previous learning and Thomas Edison State College and Excelsior College primarily operates as assessment colleges. In addition, ACE offers credentialing for diversity and inclusion leadership training.

Steps	Activity	Value Added
External Credentialing		
1. Identify Stakeholders	Curriculum for External Credentialing • Meet with external representatives and identify the criterion needed for certification, fees for all services	• Build rapport and collaboration • Get every head in the game • Establishes a competitive advantage
2. Develop Project Plan, Goals and Objectives	• Review and or develop objectives and concepts and scripts to ensure that each fall within all required criterion and are competency based • Modify (or develop curriculum) • Present curriculum to external firm for review and feedback for credentialing	• Gather pertinent data • Strategic and tactical alignment with company vision and mission • Grooming and growing leadership for national and international roles • Transference of knowledge into behaviors
3. Determine training needs (new curriculum development) or identify current current curriculum strengths	• Consider company culture when determining the methodology for content delivery (See value-added section) • Engage companywide communications plans	
1. Determine collection data methodology i.e., manual or HRIS	• Budgetary and human resources considerations	
1. Define levels of certification (awareness, knowledge, skills and experiential)	• Consider rolling all D&I training into the certification process including learning labs, videos, webinars and signature programs. Determine level for each offerings	

Template: Companywide D&I Training

External Credentialing

Date:	ERG Name:	Team Members:
Focus:	Content Level:	Content Area:

Assessment – Current Curriculum

- Strengths:
- Weaknesses:
- Opportunities:
- Threats:

External Credentialing

Goals and Objectives For Training
- Goals:
- Objectives

Vendor Certification Discussions
- Concepts & Theory Requirements for Continuing Education Credits
- Other Requirements and Changes Needed for Certification:

Updates, Reviews and Follow-up with Vendor
- Actual Updates to Curriculum:

---

10 Continuing Education credits may be used for other certifications such as SHRM

External Credentialing
Certification or Recertification of Past Participants (Considerations)
Training Processes:
Technology:
Communications:

(Integration)

Notable Mention: Most organizations offer anywhere from 4-hour to an 8-hour baseline diversity learning sessions. In instances whereby the training focuses on awareness, then the certifications would be for 4-hour (or 8-hour I&D) awareness. The area for growth would be the development and certification of future, more advanced knowledge based training. Determinants for future I&D Leadership training would take into consideration components such as levels in the organization, job description and frequency and levels of D&I disconnects (issues) within the leader's scope of responsibility. This is where ERG offerings can offset duplication training efforts, making these courses requirements for required groups.

Internal Certifications

The internal certification process template mirrors the external certification process. However, there is a noteworthy difference. In the case of the internal certification, the organization itself would certify the learning through credentialing. Thus, similar to McDonalds University, top-quality content must be included to gain respect from the organization and educational (including continuing education) industries.

Additionally, an emphasis must be placed on assessing the learning. Assessments need not be a lengthy or costly process. Partnering with current resources, internal employee development departments and HRIS systems to develop assessment tools and capture project and report results through HRIS is simply a win-win.

Assessments of participants learning and evaluations by far is where most organizations miss opportunities. It's great to have fun during training sessions. I for one am all for that. It is wonderful to have interactions with your peers in a class; discussions raise the bar for learning. It is important to embed concepts into the minds and hearts of employees so that they know what they're looking at when they see it. Inclusion is a verb, so it takes action; it takes practice to transform an organization to a knowledge base, action oriented culture. That is the goal after all for ERGs and departments of responsible for inclusion making everyone responsible and accountable for inclusion. This increases successful performance for inclusion.

Concept 2: Employee Resources Groups Certifications

ERG certification engages employees based on their interests and perhaps based on their membership. I highly recommend this certification process to be voluntary. By being voluntary employees can select to engage with some or all of the resource groups. To a greater extent they may determine whether they want to pursue a certification or merely take some of the courses provided. Moreover, it is optimal for each ERG s to voluntarily develop or recommend components for training certifications, company practices really determine how data will be collected and disseminated.

Determine baseline focuses:

- Awareness;
- Knowledge;
- Skills (including experiential); and
- Transference (to workplace).

Identify and develop key:

- Objectives and
- Learning Points.

Determine which methodologies will be used for the certifications. Here are a few recommendations:

- Webinars and Online Courses;
- Gamification – from online, to board games, quiz shows or print data;
- Experiential exercises;
- Focus Group Meetings;
- Case Studies (shorts);
- Round Table Discussions;
- Videos;
- Lunch & Learn (mini lectures);
- Storytelling;
- Observation;
- Reverse Coaching (More about this in the facilitation section); and
- Community Volunteerism.

Identify and develop concepts for each level[11] within a singular program (Office of Diversity- base level as example):

- Bias, stereotypes, prejudice, and unconscious bias (awareness);
- Generations, Gender and Cross-cultural Communications (Knowledge);
- Constructive Feedback, Listening Skills and Emotional Intelligence (Knowledge);

---

11 Recommend entry level hosted by Office of Diversity or some other overall category as some concepts must be understood (bias, stereotypes etc.,) prior to engaging ERGs

Determine means for collecting pertinent data[12]:

- Technology;
- Manual – if so, who and how data will be collected and maintained; and/or
- Hybrid – a mixture of the two.

Some methodologies are better suited for certain topics and vice-versa. I highly recommend the use of gamification for disseminating information for each ERG. Games are a great way to provide information, such as definitions, and engage participants exponentially.

Rewards for entry level and mid-level participation and successful progression and attainment of credentialing may be awarded items such as printed wristbands (multicolor denoting ERG), lapel pins and any other insignia that demonstrates to the organization participation levels and rates.

Observation and experiential learning may be demonstrated through games such as bingo, "ride public transportation and notice what you notice," or "visit a senior facility and lead an activity or take your pet with you for a visit," or "for one full day, use a different hand to write with and post some of your work." Each of these exercises for the bingo game are experiential and solidify learning, albeit a small window, into socio-economic differences, age, and one-up one down (difficulties left-handed people may experience on a daily basis).

Round table and focus group meetings may be used for potentially more intense topics and require a highly skilled facilitator. Workplaces, as humans, are not immune from society or from being human. Topics that fall under "critical mass[13]" community issues will show up in the workplace. It is far better for the company to be proactive than reactive. Strategically focused discussing sound doctrines in a proactive manner

---

12 This is an important component as it is important for benchmarking, projections and gauging participation (up to date data on how many are in the certification process, at what level, in what locations and median frequency of completion etc.,)

13 Human characteristics that evoke a strong emotional reactions such as race, religion, sexual orientation and politics

rather than allowing the issues to surface and responding reactively will serve both the organization and the company.

Concept 3: Internal I&D Facilitators

The role of a facilitator is to serve as a guide, set the stage for learning and to provide concepts (training) at various intervals of a session. Humanity or I&D, facilitation is serious business. Participants are entrusting their innermost value, beliefs and thoughts to the group including facilitators. As such, because of our differences, the inclusion of everyone can create touch points or flashpoints, real heat.

Facilitation is skill based. The more difficult the subject, the more advanced skillsets a facilitator must possess. Inclusion facilitators must be highly qualified and experienced. Organizations must be careful in engaging employee as inclusion facilitators solely because they have the desire. It is easier than one think to quickly move from a champion to a warrior on your soapbox. Or, even more harmful, when an inclusion facilitator does not have baseline knowledge of terminology and definitions, an inability to recognize landmines or historical context.

Many organizations engage their ERG members as facilitators. Thus, this is the reasoning for its inclusion here. If organizations are raising the knowledge bar companywide, then the knowledge and experiential bar of its facilitators must grow as well, at a quicker pace and deeper level than those they will serve. Below, is a short-list of skills required for facilitators.

Facilitator Requisite Skills

Listening Skills	Empathy	Ask Questions
Foster Trust	Awareness of Others	Self-Awareness
Emotional Intelligence	Flexibility	Communication
Open-Minded	Life-Long Learner	Role Model Behaviors

Both/And Thinkers Ability	Group Dynamics	Classroom Management
Abilities to Paraphrase	Adult Learning Theories	Planning
Cross Cultural Skills	Presentation Skills	Ability to Summarize
Related Personal Experiences	Related Professional Experiences	Provide Constructive Feedback

Facilitator Certification

Facilitators should receive I&D certifications that are based on three levels: basic, advanced and expert level. Obviously, each level should have specific skillset criterion and specific trainings accreditation in order to be eligible to teach based on said certifications. Each level should also be a progressive process, unless the facilitator has past verifiable experiences. In short, facilitators for inclusion must be properly vetted.

Here is one example of why certifications based on proficiency levels for facilitators are important.

An internal facilitator was promoted to a higher D&I (diversity is the emphasis within the organization) role. During a roundtable discussion of approximately 20 employees, it became quite evident that she did not know the difference between biases and stereotypes. Sadly, she could only come up with personal examples involving how animals are treated and not personal examples of people. People of color in the room began giving each other the side eye. Some had sidebars with the consultant stating, "and she was just promoted to a director role. It never ceases."

As before, this facilitator is a good person, well connected and wanted to become an active part of bringing change to the workplace. Here are some major issues:

1. Credibility, or lack thereof, for the facilitator and the organization. If a facilitator cannot demonstrate basic tenets for

understanding issues that impact people that are "other" than how can you adequately facilitate a conversation? Whether the company recognizes or acknowledges it, they sent a strong message diminishing the value of inclusion and diversity by placing an individual with limited knowledge in a high ranking role (position and relational) and in the role of a facilitator (position and relational);

2. Promoting individuals to I&D facilitation roles because they are well connected or liked impacts the quality of the selection and delivery processes. In the case of facilitators the process should without exception be based on meritocracy grounded in sound principles and skillsets;

3. Having the desire does not necessarily make for an effective facilitator. The practice of allowing someone to facilitate because they have a desire is a common practice and a typical mistake. One can have the heart and compassion for diversity and quickly move from an agent of change to an agent of confusion and anger when they are on the floor facilitating especially when they are unaware or don't understand concepts or experiences beyond their own. There have been instances where I&D facilitators have become so wrapped up in their own "baggage," or step so high on their soapbox that they breakdown, point fingers, attack or refute. These actions go against the tenets of facilitation;

4. You cannot teach that which you do not know. Firstly, you must do the work to begin knowing yourself. If you are unable to do this, then you are unable to facilitate topics on human and social issues. To facilitate humanity discussions one must have a huge helping of Emotional Intelligence (EI). To facilitate inclusion and diversity one does not always need firsthand experiences – I have no clue what it is really like to be a white woman. I am however willing to be open to learning. One must be positioned to demonstrate empathy, know what questions to ask and when without judgment or heat, be able to say I don't know and not make up an inanimate example to explain away a human condition. One must do their own work in self-discovery coupled with

learning sound concepts and have the ability to connect everything to human experiences.

This is hugely important for inclusion and diversity facilitators. There are people working in organizations who do not feel valued, who are not able to contribute, who are shown through actions that inclusion and diversity are purely programs. For these and other reasons facilitators must engage participants in such a way that they feel safe, are able to share – even share counterpoints to prevailing organizational thought to avoid groupthink and assist with identifying and tearing down walls of exclusion.

Examples of inclusion and diversity training that would fall within basic, advanced and expert level training:

- Basic – Generations, Gender (awareness), and concepts such as entry-level terminology: constructive feedback, bias and stereotypes.
- Advanced – Cross-Culture Communications, Microinequities, Simultaneity and more advanced concepts and theories.
- Expert Level – Race, Religion, Sexual Orientation, Intersectionality, ethnocentrism and a confluence of concepts and theories that have been internalized more so than memorized.

Facilitators are the first responders for organizations. They are the ambassadors for respecting and valuing the human condition while cultivating an environment for members to practice self-actualization. Facilitators should be positioned to serve a dual purpose. Here is a concept that many organizations have not capitalized on:

Reverse Coaching

Facilitators should also be trained to coach leaders on inclusion and diversity concerns and thoughts that they may have. There is a distinct difference between offering human resources solutions and coaching. Usually human resources would be called upon when there is a problem. Some organizations have updated their human resources departments to move from a transactional organization to a consultative one. This is admirable and forward thinking. Of course, HR, if adequately trained, can fulfill the role of an inclusion and diversity coach, unfortunately this blurred line may be difficult for stakeholders to accept. On one hand you are disciplining me and now you want to be my coach. Will I provide you enough information to use against me? These sentiments posed by employees may come up for internal HR representatives whether they are voiced or not.

Reverse coaching permit those facilitators with significant experience to coach leaders rather than the other way around. Leaders can some times be at a disadvantage. Many may not have firsthand knowledge or experience to effectively manage inclusion and diversity on the level that is needed because of privilege (there are all kinds of privileges racial, gender, socio-economic, position in the organization etc.) and in this case status. Moreover, if leaders make certain statements, even though they may be speaking in their truth, just as the facilitator example provided earlier, the remarks most likely will become folklore. And some folklore can hamper relationships, create interpersonal and leadership disconnects and undermine authority.

There are numerous evolving trends that have direct impact on leaders, managers and supervisors. One significant change is how they interact with personnel. Culturally the role of managers and supervisors shifted from "being the boss and telling people what to do," working within a group that primarily looked like you, thought like you (and if you don't keep it to yourself), and had similar expectations and behaviors. There are numerous trends that have shifted the role of an employee. Current organizations seek talent that is self-directed, accountable for their actions, innovative, and willing to expand their roles. In short, organizations necessitate teamwork, collaboration and communicating with people who may have different experiences, expectations and behaviors. Managing talent that is different requires different skillsets that will not happen through osmosis. Facilitators are positioned to augment growing leaders, managers and supervisors.

Trustworthy facilitators are bound by confidentiality and are unique resources that will gain a great deal from learning to coach inclusion and diversity leaders who will immediately transfer their knowledge back to the organization. Most, facilitators know that participants often stay after class, including leaders, and ask "real-world" questions seeking assistance. Why not put it to great use, and certify facilitators as inclusion and diversity coaches. Naturally the roles of the coach will need to have clear standards, parameters and role descriptions.

Concept 4: ERGs Intersectionality and Simultaneity Certifications

If need be refer back to the definitions for intersectionality and simultaneity prior to reading through this certification process. In many ways intersectionality is simplistic and in many ways it is not because there are a multitude of variations.

Implementation of this concept into an ERG initiative serves several very important strategies (1) This process will crack open the door between the silo structure of ERGs allowing the pairing and collaboration between two or more groups. This process strategy also creates interdependence. (2) It addresses more of the full essence of people and the issues they may be confronted with – similarly to the changes to the census data in FY2000 (3) it raises the bar on awareness and understanding. It bring to light to those who may have blind spots or blinders on situations that create exclusion (4) It builds trust within an organization (5) It will truly demonstrate how dynamic social identities are.

Many organizations engage in events to highlight ERGs internally. Some events are year-end or beginning year kickoff events, some are regional meetings and or leadership events. If your organization does not comport these type strategies now might be a great time to evaluate and consider; this section will provide you food for thought.

In the intersectionality certification process your goal is to conduct a hybrid training or event, and present, at a minimum, two different sessions, once per year. Identify 4-6 employee resources groups to work in pairs and develop a key learning. The key learning may be presented as table topics discussions or focus group meetings or learning lab.

As an example, partner the Women's Group with the Hispanic Latino group (impacts of the glass ceiling for Latina Women), pair African American resource group with LGBT resource group (as example, being black and gay man), or pair Generations resource group from the U.S.

and another country site and discuss nuances. After all, many of these employees are interfacing with international peers and may be missing the mark in communications (yes, communicating through technology counts).

Concept 5: Capstones

Capstones may be offered in the final level for an ERG certification. Or it may be an overall final level after all ERG certifications has been attained. However, the latter may be too far apart for the learning, the goal is to transfer the knowledge to practice as close to the learning as possible. For this reason it's a good idea to use mini-fun assessments closer to the learning and end users will not feel as if they are being set up for failure. In any case, an assessment should be used to capture and reinforce learning.

Capstones may also be used to reinforce global learning gained throughout the process (using statistical data and culture understanding for countries where the organization has site locations to make it relevant) and/or capstones may be used to drill down key company messages and/or internal policies concerning inclusion.

When implementing capstones in addition to being educational make it fun, interactive and worthwhile. However, don't make it too fun and too easy – inclusion is serious business as it is an imperative for all organizations and its members. Keep the learning in the forefront.

Getting Started

There is a great deal of information within these pages on creating and implementing certification processes. A great deal of information was intentionally left out of this quick book to avoid creating tunnel vision or a limiting mindset. It is important that you create your own. Each organization's culture is different and thus each certification process must be developed for the end users based on objectives, goals and mission. How you get started in the certification process is equally as important as the journey itself.

Change management professionals understand the need to take measured steps before making full-scale changes or any change that will impact the entire organization. The absolute best place to start is through building relationships as you build your certification strategy.

Internal Partnerships

Gaining buy-in from inception to implementation forward is fundamental. The more people are allowed to give input the more stake they have in working towards successful performance. Employees are great resources for providing topical issues that are important to them and to the culture of the organization. After all, partnerships are about inclusion and a great way to begin to explore simultaneity and intersectionality. Some partnerships to involve and stay in communication with are listed below alphabetically.

- ERG Members
- Human Resources / Office of Diversity
- IT
- Leadership
- Training and Development, and
- Other stakeholders

There are several strategies to introduce certifications into the organization and build relationships. Here are a few:

1. Establish a baseline accrediting learning for the overall inclusion strategy. Phase ERGs into the process (view upcoming certification model following this section);
2. Focus on quick hits and beginning with an overall Office of Inclusion certification process establishing baseline learning such as diversity and inclusion definitions, self-discovery, learning about others. I am a staunch proponent of self as a learning tool and others as a learning tool. Develop four or five quick hit courses to engage the overall organization and raise awareness, provide knowledge and opportunity to practice. The governing body (office of diversity or HR) should not steal the thunder or undercut ERGs inclusion focus. Meaning, in the overarching

baseline introduction course into ERG certifications, do not offer learning on topics that they would cover (women, LGBT and so forth). Instead focus on those things that make everyone human;
3. Focus in on each ERG and evaluate the services that they currently offer and determine how these learning could be included in an overall certification process. Determine current trainings being offered and assess whether the training is a beginner, mid-level or advanced course. Determine which tier the course is applicable to the certification process and include it in a course outline. This option is a great way to provide credits for learning already established;
4. Multinational companies must seek ways to partner with their counterparts in other countries. Be sure to use these partnerships when building the global components. Here is an example, "Did You Know," use this game or webinar to communicate key information that the "national" would want you to know more so than what we think we should know. In other words, "here is what we want Americans to know about us" and vice-versa.

This next model is a visual tool based on strategies that were introduced in earlier chapters. The next few pages, beginning with the certification strategy model will provide more intellectual food for thought beginning.

Certification Strategy Model

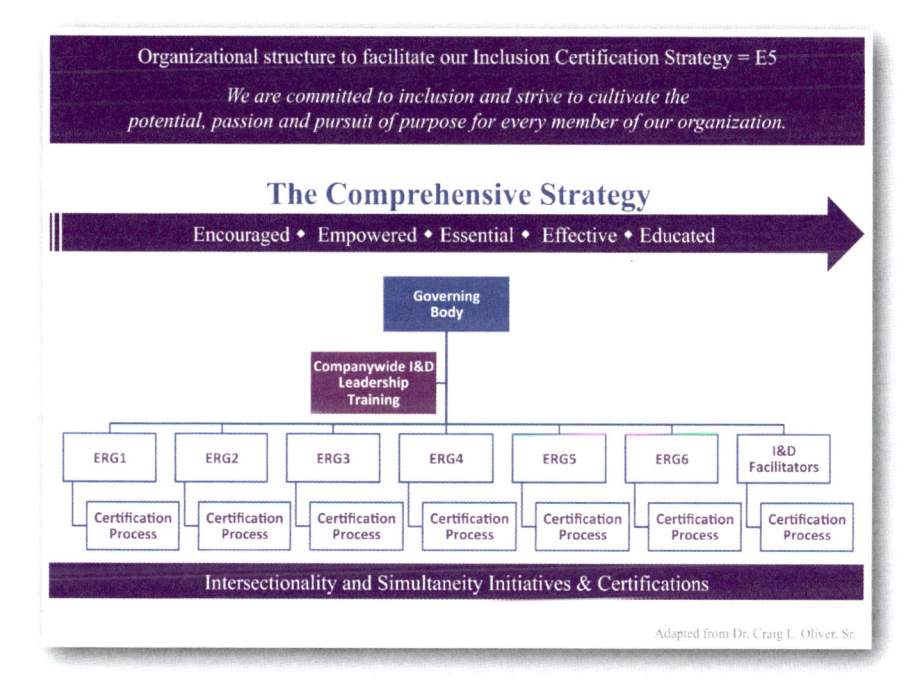

Organizational structure to facilitate our Inclusion Certification Strategy = E5

We are committed to inclusion and strive to cultivate the potential, passion and pursuit of purpose for every member of our organization.

The Comprehensive Strategy

Encouraged ◆ Empowered ◆ Essential ◆ Effective ◆ Educated

- Governing Body
  - Companywide I&D Leadership Training
    - ERG1 — Certification Process
    - ERG2 — Certification Process
    - ERG3 — Certification Process
    - ERG4 — Certification Process
    - ERG5 — Certification Process
    - ERG6 — Certification Process
    - I&D Facilitators — Certification Process

Intersectionality and Simultaneity Initiatives & Certifications

Adapted from Dr. Craig L. Oliver, Sr.

Low Hanging Fruit

This section provides several strategies that will aid in the creation of a continuous learning environment.

Value-Added Actions

Examples of Certificate and Pledge

Two highly visible tools to use to recognize and reward accomplishments are a certificate and pledge.

Certifications are a visible form of accomplishment. Not every employee wants to be rewarded in front of everyone. Yet, for those whom do, they are able to place the certifications on their desk, on the wall, in their lockers. In fact both certifications and pledges may be displayed in the workplace or at home. Be sure to include the number of hours that has been invested by the participant. Certificates can be developed and printed internally. However, certificates should be of high quality to indicate the value of higher learning.

Pledges are a great way to reinforce commitment and focus employees on the value of being inclusive. Pledges signal to the masses that this is a higher calling. Pledges motivate. There is no need to have different pledges for different employee resources group. The pledge is the unifier between the employee resources groups, another way to fuse the groups and blur the lines of silos.

Wording for both the pledge and certifications are key communication tool. Use it to attract employees internally so that they will willingly engage in the certification process.

AWARENESS TRAINING CERTIFICATE

CONTINUING EDUCATION FOR LGBT INCLUSION

Congratulations on becoming certified as a LGBT Awareness Ally. This certificate demonstrates your commitment to continued intellectual, professional and personal EXCELLENCE. We recognize your successful completion of 4.5 hours Inclusion and Diversity Continuous Learning Program focusing on the human dimension of sexual orientation CERTIFIED AWARENESS ALLY

IS AWARDED TO

[Insert Name]

XYZ COMPANY

[INSERT DATE]

_____
[NAME, TITLE]

_____
[NAME, TITLE]

Learn • Experiential • Knowledge • Transference to Workplace • Transform

INCLUSIONIST PLEDGE

I, _____, believe in the principles of inclusionism, a holistic approach to recognizing the value of human beings to live meaningful lives and contribute fully individually and collectively in their personal and professional community.

I will engage with my fellow cohorts, customers, clients and other stakeholders to create an environment where everyone is able to contribute fully with all of their talents, skills, abilities and gifts that they possess. In fulfilling this pledge, I demonstrate my commitment to furthering our company goals of valuing, respecting, and leveraging inclusion.

To that end, I pledge to:

- Become a lifelong learner on inclusion principles
- Participate in learning activities;
- Give of myself to others to help them grow and learn as they, too, assist me in growing and learning;
- Practice inclusive behaviors including listening to the opinions, thoughts and ideas of others;
- Represent the change in the world that I wish to see; and
- Support the mission and vision of inclusion

In the event that I fall short as an inclusion role model, I humbly invite others to provide me constructive feedback, engage respectfully with me in crucial conversations, and assist me as an ally, ambassador, role model and agent of change. I will treat others in kind.

_____   _____
Name   Date

Value-Added Actions
Creating pathways for employee to connect, learn, have fun and transfer their knowledge to the workplace and the communities they serve in is always a winning strategy.

- Create and implement a course catalogue or handbook (either hardcopy or electronic). The catalogue or handbook, similar to university catalogues, should provide a background on the concepts and theories that will be discussed, what courses are required (including prerequisites), expected timing to fulfill the course and every actions needed to successfully complete the process and receive certification and or any other completion award. In addition, if assessments will be required it should be so noted in the handbook. Be sure to include a frequently asked question (FQA) section and highlight upfront each ERGs program (accomplishments, milestones, goals and mission), identifying how to become a member if an employee so chooses;
- D&I Journals –An excellent learning tool for individuals to capture their thoughts and discover, acknowledge and act upon their own experiential and course learning, biases, fears, and concerns etc. This is also a great way to motivate and inspire individuals to engage in continuous learning. To drive the learning the design of the journal may include quotes, thoughts of the day, and spaces for pledges or to do lists. I am a proponent of journals. In most of my offerings I provide journals. Here's the deal, a journal may be optional and thus participants elect not to engage. If a participant elects to not use the journal (and it is required) they take it home and someone else just might use it. Journals may also be a mandatory component of the certification process; it is beneficial for each of us to engage in self-reflection and use our reflections as a learning tool;
- Group Text - daily or weekly inspirational thought provoking quotes to employees in the certification process;
- Create an Internal I&D Webpage (similar to Facebook) asking members to post ways that they celebrated or acknowledge

holidays or celebrations i.e., Veteran's Day, Women History Month and so forth and perhaps post thoughts for today;

- Develop an App for inclusion downloadable by internal employees only. Companies cannot ignore the current popularity of Apps in our society;
- Develop and implement online assessments for each capstone. This ensures that learning is taking place (if HRIS systems cannot accommodate the new program or is too costly to create use tools such as Survey Monkey);
- Use color-coded certificates to indicate tier learning such as bronze (beginner), silver (intermediary), and gold (proficient);
- Seriously consider using gamifications to deliver messages, especially messages that can be deemed boring by end users such as definitions…replace boring with anticipation and fun is a win-win. Contrary to popular beliefs, adults do love games and partnered with technology games are readily accessible. Examples include Bingo, Did You Know, Family Feud, Jeopardy and much, much more;
- Once again, if at all possible, use IT to build processes electronically. This way the organization will readily be able to download crucial information for reports including day-to-day and annual, collate information with AAPs (affirmative action plans), highlights areas for the number of participants amongst other things. Remember the old adage, what gets measured, gets done!

Epilogue

Inclusion and diversity is a major influencer in organizations all over the world. And as such many companies view inclusion as a strategic imperative – it is. In an effort to incorporate all of the talents, skillsets, thought leadership and knowledge into the workforce and enhance their brands companies must continuously seek comprehensive strategies that add value. Generations are faced with a new world and we must be able to infuse not only the best and brightest but everyone that is willing to give their best and brightest.

Because organizations are wonderfully comprised of people who have different histories, experiences, backgrounds, unique stories and other human characteristics; people must remain at the heart of the organization. We must ardently strive to create winds of uplifting spirits, of connecting, of valuing, of interpreting what is important to one another. This can and must be done through our people strategies. Employee Resources Groups is but one of those strategies. ERGs bring forth the hopes and desires of its people. History has shown that hopes and desires propel positive energies and synergies.

Risk-taking, innovation, flexibility, and expanding global territories yield growth. Multinationals continues to build bridges to various cultures, lands, commerce, and people. Investing in people through employee resource groups yields ample opportunities and growth and minimizes risks to employee relations, lessens the opportunity for disconnects which in turn will positively impact organizational performance while bringing people closer to their purpose.

Everything evolves – people, places and things. It is natural, organic for employee resources groups to retain certain elements, outgrow others and give birth to new idealism. Certification processes will assist the organization to grow as a living, breathing learning environment.

Employee Resources Groups really is about valuing people, impacting performance and transforming organizations and communities in which they serve and live.

About the Author

Nyah Lynn Edwards is the founder and CEO of Nyah Lynn & Associates, keynote speaker, trainer and facilitator. She is a leader in creating and implementing strategies addressing organizational and individual behavior including talent development, coaching, and curriculum development. She has coached individuals from the frontline to C-suite. Nyah Lynn is passionate about cultivating and reviving the potential in every individual as they move along their personal and organizational growth continuum. She has worked with a variety of industries including education, government (both city and federal), utility (gas, electric and nuclear), healthcare, facility management and construction in addition to others. She has amassed years of experience and insights into organizational work-life. Nyah Lynn holds a M.S. in Organizational Change and Leadership, Pfeiffer University of Charlotte, North Carolina and B.S. in Management, University of Illinois, and Springfield. Nyah Lynn is author of, "*I'm Just Saying: When Women Misbehave in the Workplace*," and co-author of "*Ten Business Reasons Organizations Fail at Race Relations.*" Ms. Edwards hosts a blog for and about women – Ask Nyah Lynn & Sister Friends; this blog reaches women in 20+ countries.

If you are interested in getting started with developing certification processes for Employee Resources Groups or other strategies for D&I, you may contact Ms. Edwards at:

Nyahlynnassociates.com
nyahlynnassociates@gmail.com

Edited by Dr. Bernardine Conner, owner of Dorcas Reading Institute
Book Cover by Maria Klein Holdren, owner of Holdren Design.
Cover photo by Shutterstock ©.
Graphics and book design by Sheila Oien, owner of WriteDesign

Made in the USA
Lexington, KY
15 August 2019